101 Facts About Our World
101 Facts About

101 FACTS ABOUT

RIVERS

Julia Barnes

Gareth Stevens Publishing
A WORLD ALMANAC EDUCATION GROUP COMPANY

Please visit our web site at: www.garethstevens.com
For a free color catalog describing Gareth Stevens Publishing's
list of high-quality books and multimedia programs,
call 1-800-542-2595 (USA) or 1-800-387-3178 (Canada).
Gareth Stevens Publishing's fax: (414) 332-3567.

Library of Congress Cataloging-in-Publication Data

Barnes, Julia, 1955-
    101 facts about rivers / by Julia Barnes. — North American ed.
        p. cm. — (101 facts about our world)
    Summary: Describes the characteristics, formation, uses, plant and animal life,
and conservation of rivers.
    Includes bibliographical references and index.
    ISBN 0-8368-3711-8 (lib. bdg.)
    1. Stream ecology—Juvenile literature. 2. Rivers—Juvenile literature. [1. Rivers.
2. Stream ecology. 3. Ecology.] I. Title: One hundred one facts about rivers.
II. Title: One hundred and one facts about rivers. III. Title: Rivers. IV. Title.
QH541.5.S7B37   2003
551.48′3—dc21   2003045710

This North American edition first published in 2004 by
Gareth Stevens Publishing
A World Almanac Education Group Company
330 West Olive Street, Suite 100
Milwaukee, WI 53212 USA

This U.S. edition copyright © 2004 by Gareth Stevens, Inc. Original edition © 2003 by First
Stone Publishing. First published by First Stone Publishing, 4/5 The Marina, Harbour
Road, Lydney, Gloucestershire, GL15 5ET, United Kingdom. Additional end matter © 2004
by Gareth Stevens, Inc.

First Stone Series Editor: Claire Horton-Bussey
First Stone Designer: Rob Benson
Geographical consultant: Miles Ellison
Gareth Stevens Editors: Catherine Gardner and JoAnn Early Macken

Photographs © Oxford Scientific Films Ltd

Printed in Hong Kong through Printworks Int. Ltd

1 2 3 4 5 6 7 8 9 07 06 05 04 03

For most of us, good, clean water never seems too far away. Most of the water on Earth, however, is the saltwater of oceans, which humans cannot drink. We must rely on the water from lakes and rivers, which is called freshwater, to give us water to drink, to grow crops, and to supply electric power. It makes sense to take care of our rivers, but all too often, people allow rivers to become **polluted**. People change the courses of rivers to make them more usable, but the changes are not always good for rivers or for the wildlife that depends on them.

People need rivers in order to survive. Rivers also provide homes to many kinds of plants and animals. Now is the time for us to protect our rivers, before it is too late.

MAJOR RIVERS OF THE WORLD

Mackenzie

Yukon

NORTH AMERICA

Okanagan

St. Lawrence

North Pacific Ocean

Columbia

Snake

Ohio

North Atlantic Ocean

Missouri

Colorado

Mississippi

Rio Grande

Magdalena

Orinoco

São Francisco

South Pacific Ocean

Amazon

SOUTH AMERICA

South Atlantic Ocean

Paraguay

Paraná

Uruguay

Key

EUROPEAN RIVERS

1. Rhine
2. Thames
3. Shannon
4. Seine
5. Loire
6. Rhone
7. Po
8. Danube

Permanent ice caps

Principal rivers

Division between North and South America

Division between Asia and Africa

Division between Europe and Asia

Division between Asia and Oceania

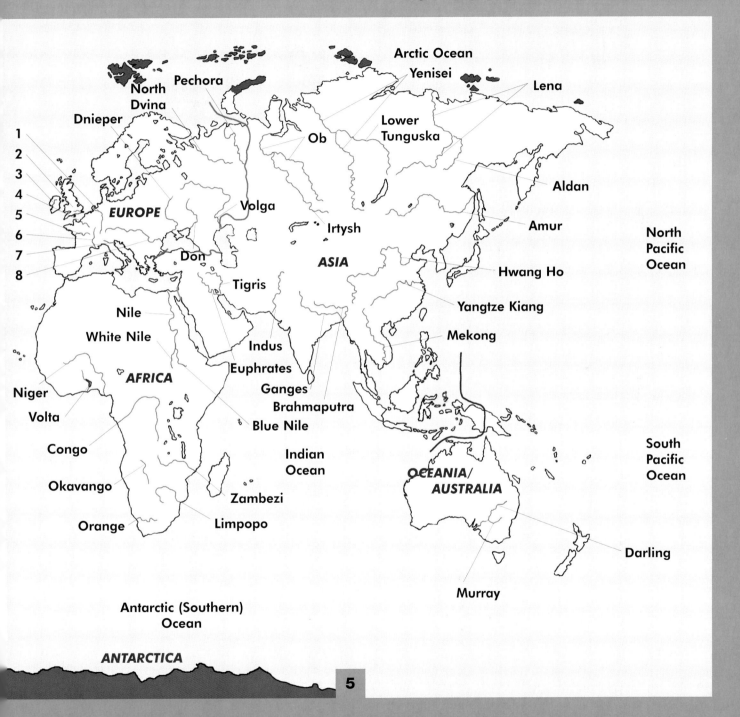

Arctic Ocean

Yenisei

Lena

Pechora

North
Dvina

Dnieper

Lower
Tunguska

Ob

Aldan

1
2
3
4
5
6
7
8

Volga

EUROPE

Irtysh

Amur

North
Pacific
Ocean

Don

ASIA

Hwang Ho

Tigris

Yangtze Kiang

Nile

White Nile

Indus

Mekong

AFRICA

Euphrates

Ganges

Niger

Brahmaputra

Volta

Blue Nile

Indian
Ocean

Congo

OCEANIA/
AUSTRALIA

South
Pacific
Ocean

Okavango

Zambezi

Orange

Limpopo

Darling

Murray

Antarctic (Southern)
Ocean

ANTARCTICA

1 About two-thirds of Earth's surface is water, but most of it is seawater.

2 Humans need to drink freshwater, not the salty seawater found in oceans and seas.

3 Most of the freshwater on Earth forms the ice sheets of the North and South Poles, and it is frozen all year long.

4 Rivers and lakes also contain freshwater, but they make up just 1 percent of all the water on Earth.

5 Sometimes people build huge **dams** (below) and **reservoirs** along rivers so they can more easily use the water for drinking, washing, growing crops, and making electric power.

8 In the past, people often followed the paths of rivers to explore new parts of the world.

6 We cannot live without freshwater, so people often settle near rivers. Some settlements grow into large cities. The city of London, England, grew up along the Thames River (above).

9 People use rivers to travel to different places and to move things from one place to another.

7 Animals and plants need freshwater, too. Rivers and riverbanks are home to many different kinds of wildlife.

of a person, who goes from childhood to old age.

12 Rivers always start on high ground. From there, they run downward, either to a lake or to an ocean. Along the way, rivers grow deeper and wider.

10 The longest river in the world is the Nile River (above) in Africa. It is more than 4,160 miles (6,690 kilometers) long.

11 A river has many stages from its start in the hills to its end near the sea. You might think of the stages of a river like the life

13 When the Amazon River reaches the end of its journey in Brazil, South America, it pours nearly 29 million gallons (110 million liters) of water into the ocean every second.

14 Even rivers as large as the Amazon start out as a tiny trickle.

15 The starting point of a river is called the **source** (right).

16 A river may start with water from an underground spring or with the melting snow of glaciers high up in the mountains.

17 As the water starts to flow down the steep slopes, it becomes a small stream and cuts a channel in the rock.

18 Other small streams, called tributaries, may join the main flow of water. As more tributaries join the main river, the river becomes wider, deeper, and more powerful.

19 At its start, a river is as full of energy as a child. It tumbles over rocks and races along the ground.

22 If a river passes over high ground, it can cut a narrow valley with sides like steep cliffs. This kind of valley is called a river gorge.

20 Water can carve a narrow, steep-sided **valley** (above) in the land. A valley forms the shape of the letter V.

21 As the water rushes along the ground, it picks up sand, gravel, and small rocks, which can help the water **erode** deep paths, called channels.

23 The largest river gorge in the world is the Grand Canyon (right), which is located in Arizona in the southwestern United States. The Colorado River made this mighty canyon by wearing away layers of rock.

24 The Grand Canyon is up to 18 miles (29 km) wide in some spots. It is 277 miles (446 km) long and more than one mile (1.6 km) deep. Some of the rocks at the bottom of this huge gorge are two billion years old.

25 The river took five million years to carve the Grand Canyon.

26 When a river flows over a ledge of hard rock, the water spills over the edge. This action creates a waterfall.

27 One of the most famous waterfalls in the world is Niagara Falls (below). On the border of Canada and the United States, it carries water from Lake Erie to Lake Ontario.

28 Angel Falls in Venezuela has the longest drop in the world, plunging down an amazing 3,212 feet (979 meters).

29 If a river goes over or around large rocks, it creates an area of shallow, fast-flowing water called **rapids** (right).

30 The water in rapids rushes at such speed that it could easily smash a boat to bits against the rocks.

31 Some people enjoy going down rapids on special kinds of rafts or narrow boats such as canoes or kayaks. It is an exciting and dangerous sport.

34 The torrent duck can brace itself against rocks with a long, stiff-quilled tail. It holds on with tiny spurs at the "wrists" of its wings.

32 Most plants are not able to grow roots in the rapids, and few animals can survive in the fast-flowing water.

35 Finding food in the rushing water of the rapids is hard. The torrent duck eats tiny insect larvae.

33 The torrent duck (right), which lives along part of the Amazon River in South America, is one bird that has found a special way to live and find food in fast-flowing water.

13

36 It is hard enough to stay still in rapids, but salmon (above) are great swimmers and acrobats. These fish manage to travel up and down the rapids.

37 Salmon hatch from eggs. After feeding for a couple of weeks, they swim down the river, making their way over waterfalls and through rapids.

38 Salmon swim down the whole course of the river until they reach the ocean, where they stay until they are ready to breed.

39 After breeding, they leave the ocean and go back up the river. This time, the salmon must swim against the strong flow of the water.

40 Atlantic salmon can leap over waterfalls up to 9 feet (2.7 m) high.

41 Salmon finish their incredible journey exactly where it started – at the place in the river where the salmon hatched. New salmon are now born, and the adult fish die.

42 As the river leaves the mountains, the valley becomes wider, and the sides are less steep. This is known as the **middle course** of the river.

43 The water in the middle course of the river moves more slowly than the water at the source.

44 As it swings around a bend, a river erodes the soil of the far bank and dumps sand and stone on the inner bank.

45 The bend, which is called a meander (below), gets bigger, and in time, the river flows in a series of loops in a much wider valley.

48 A meander can grow until only a thin strip of land is left between the bends in the river.

49 Water takes the easiest route. Sometimes it cuts through a meander to form a new, straighter channel.

46 The Mississippi River in the United States has so many meanders that American writer Mark Twain called it the "crookedest river in the world."

47 As time goes by, a meander grows so wide that it is shaped almost like a circle.

50 When a river cuts through a meander, it leaves a horseshoe-shaped lake called an **oxbow lake** (left). An oxbow lake dries up after a period of time, but it may refill if the river floods.

51 Soil that erodes from the banks of the river travels in the water as tiny mud particles. This soil provides important **nutrients** that help plants grow under the water and along the riverbanks.

52 Butterflies (below), dragonflies, and other insects live among plants along the riverbank.

53 The water in a river, which is warmer than water in a deep lake, produces plenty of food for many different kinds of fish.

54 Fish-eating birds like rivers, too. The kingfisher (below) hovers just over the surface of the water. Then it quickly dives to catch a tasty fish.

17

55 A long-necked bird called a heron fishes by standing very still. When a fish rises to the surface of the water, the heron grabs it.

56 Some animals that live near rivers are such good swimmers that they feel as much at home in the water as on the land.

57 Otters (left) are good at swimming and diving in the river. They have short, strong legs and webbed feet, and they can close their nostrils and stay underwater for as long as five minutes.

58 Some of the busiest animals along the river are beavers (above). Their strong teeth can cut down trees to build homes.

18

59 A beaver drags the trees it cuts and fallen logs it finds to make a dam across the river.

60 The beaver's dam forms a pond. The beaver then builds its home, called a lodge, in the pond.

61 Along African rivers live the hippopotamus and its small cousin, called the pygmy hippo (right). The name "hippopotamus" means "river horse."

62 During the hottest part of the day, a hippopotamus stays in the river. Only its eyes and ears show above the surface of the water.

65 A hungry crocodile grabs its prey and drags it to the river. Using its tail like a club, the crocodile can stun an animal and then drown it.

63 As the river leaves its middle course, it reaches an area of flatter land. This area is called the **lower course** of the river.

64 Crocodiles and alligators (above) lurk in the swampy water of tropical rivers. They wait for an animal to come to the river's edge for a drink.

66 Crocodiles and alligators, which are alike in many ways, often swallow stones. They may do this because the stones' weight helps them stay underwater longer.

67 Many different kinds of water rats and

mice live along riverbanks all around the world.

68 Water rats and mice all swim well, but the best swimmer of them all is the South American water rat. It can dive underwater to catch fish.

69 As a river travels far away from its source, the water runs more slowly (below). It no longer has the power to cut into the land. Instead, it gently wears away the banks.

70 The river carries fine mud and sand, known as sediment.

71 The Yellow River in China is called the muddiest river in the world. It carries more sediment than any other river.

74 The fertile soil of the floodplain is good for growing crops, but a floodplain can be a dangerous place to live (above right).

72 A heavy rain can drop more water in the river channel than it can hold. The river overflows its banks, causing a flood.

73 The land that floods when the river has too much water is called the floodplain. After a flood, the water returns to the river and leaves behind rich, **fertile** soil on the floodplain.

75 Most of the land in the southern Asian country of Bangladesh is in the floodplain of the Ganges and Brahmaputra Rivers.

76 During the rainy season, the rivers in Bangladesh flood, wrecking homes, swamping farms, and killing many people.

79 By this point, a river flows so slowly that it cannot carry sediment. It deposits, or drops, the sediment, forming **sandbanks** and **mudflats** along its course.

77 A river may end its journey by flowing into a lake. It may flow into another river that travels to a lake or the sea.

78 The place where a river joins the sea can be wide or narrow. A wide, funnel-shaped opening is an **estuary** (right). A narrow opening is a **mouth**.

81 The Mississippi River in the United States and the Ganges River in India form two large, well-known deltas.

82 Deltas make good homes for many kinds of fish. Deltas also attract lots of long-legged, long-beaked wading birds that feed on the fish in the shallow river channels.

80 As the sandbanks and mudflats grow, the river water cuts channels through the thick sediment and continues on its way to the sea. This area of river channels and sediment is called a **delta** (above).

83 For a small river, the path from its source to a lake or to a place where it joins a bigger river may be quite short.

84 Sometimes, many rivers join together to form a long system that drains a vast area of land.

85 In Canada, the Mackenzie River system includes many rivers. It drains, or carries water away from, an area that is almost as large as Mexico.

86 The huge Amazon River (below) flows across South America for 4,050 miles (6,515 km). On its way to the Atlantic Ocean, the river is joined by more than a thousand tributaries.

87 People have always needed rivers. Some of the earliest known human settlements were between two rivers in Asia, the Tigris and the Euphrates.

88 Some people try to change the paths of rivers so they can use the water or protect themselves.

89 Rivers can do a lot of damage. A river floods when too much water moves into its channel, and it cannot hold it all. Rivers may flood because of high tides, rain that is very heavy or that falls over many days, or a sudden temperature increase that melts ice and snow.

90 If the flood is very severe, a river may carry a hundred times more water than usual, and it can destroy anything in its path.

91 Dams and flood barriers (below) protect people who live near rivers from the effects of floods. For example, millions of people depend on the Thames Barrier.

92 On the Mississippi River in the United States, it has cost billions of dollars to control flooding by changing the course of the river and building **levees** to keep the water in its channel.

93 Flood-defense steps can take care of the problem for a while, but the river fights back as it tries to find the easiest path across the land (right).

94 People also have tried to change the paths of rivers to get water for their crops more easily.

95 Rivers offer a vital source of freshwater and homes to wildlife, but people are in danger of spoiling the rivers and water.

96 In some places, people take so much water that they upset the river's natural balance.

99 Waste pours out of cities and factories and off of some farm fields. All too often, this waste ends up in rivers (left).

100 Waste material pollutes our river water. Water pollution kills many kinds of plant and animal life.

97 People can hurt a river by overfishing, or fishing so much that some kinds of fish no longer live in that river.

101 We must understand how important rivers are and do everything we can to take good care of them for ourselves and for all the wildlife that needs rivers.

98 An overfished river hurts people, but it is even worse for animals with no other source of food.

Glossary

dams: structures that block a river.

delta: a low-lying, swampy area where a river meets the ocean in many narrow channels.

erode: to cut into the land.

estuary: a wide, funnel-shaped opening where a river flows into the sea.

fertile: full of the nutrients plants need to grow.

levees: artificial banks that keep the river in its channel and try to prevent flooding.

lower course: the last part of a river before it enters the sea.

middle course: the part of a river between its fast and shallow beginning and its slow-moving and deep ending.

mouth: a narrow opening where a river flows into the sea.

mudflats: flat areas that are often covered by shallow water.

nutrients: food.

oxbow lake: a horseshoe-shaped lake that forms when a meander is cut off from a river.

polluted: made dirty and unhealthy for people or wildlife.

rapids: shallow, fast-flowing water going over or around big rocks.

reservoirs: artificial lakes where water is collected and stored.

sandbanks: large areas of sand that form mounds or bars.

source: the starting point of a river.

valley: a channel cut through hills by a river.

More Books to Read

Animals of Rivers, Lakes, and Ponds
Sandra Donovan
(Raintree/Steck Vaughn)

The Big Rivers: The Missouri, the Mississippi, and the Ohio
Bruce Hiscock
(Atheneum)

Rivers and Lakes (Eye Wonder series)
Simon Holland
(Dorling Kindersley)

Rivers and Oceans (Young Discoverers series)
Barbara Taylor
(Houghton Mifflin)

Web Sites

American Rivers
www.amrivers.org/kids

River Ecology
web.bryant.edu/~langlois/ecology/riversproject.htm

River Facts
www.factmonster.com/ipka/A0001779.html

Water Science for Schools
wwwga.usgs.gov/edu/

To find additional web sites, use a reliable search engine to find one or more of the following keywords: **Amazon, river, world rivers.**

Index

alligators 20
Amazon River 8, 9, 13, 25
Angel Falls 12

beaver 18, 19
birds 13, 17, 18, 24
Brahmaputra River 22

Colorado River 10
crocodiles 20

Euphrates River 25

fish 14, 15, 17, 18, 24, 28
floodplain 22

Ganges River 22, 24
Grand Canyon 10, 11

hippopotamus 19

insects 13, 17

Mackenzie River 25
Mississippi River 16, 24, 27

Niagara Falls 12
Nile River 8

otter 18
oxbow lake 16

rapids 12, 13, 14

Thames Barrier 26
Thames River 7
Tigris River 25

waterfalls 11, 12, 14

Yellow River 21